THE GREAT INDIAN SAVINGS ADVENTURE

From Rags to Riches: A Tale of Financial Resilience

DHANDESH

Copyright © 2023 DHANDESHWARAN K S

All rights reserved.

ISBN: 9798393295967

CONTENTS

DEDICATION 04

PREFACE 05

INTRODUCTION 06

THE FAMILY CRISIS 08

THE MONEY STRUGGLE BEGINS 14

THE FAMILY MEETING 18

THE FAMILY'S MONEY-SAVING ATTEMPTS 23

THE INVESTMENT IDEA 27

THE STOCK MARKET JOURNEY 30

THE SETBACK 34

THE COMEDY OF ERRORS 37

THE GREAT INDIAN SAVINGS ADVENTURE

THE TURNING POINT **41**

A SWEET SUCCESS **46**

AFTERWARD **51**

EPILOGUE **52**

ABOUT THE AUTHOR **53**

DEDICATION

To my dear parents, who have always supported me and encouraged me to follow my dreams. Your unwavering love and guidance have been the foundation of my success.

To S.K.Buvaneshwaran and Sowmya Nadar, who have gone above and beyond to help me bring this book to life. Your design skills and attention to detail have made the cover page beautiful, and your meticulous proofreading has ensured the content is of the highest quality.

Thank you all for being a part of this journey with me. This book would not have been possible without your support and contributions.

PREFACE

Welcome to "The Great Indian Savings Adventure"! This book tells the story of the Sharma family's journey from financial struggle to stability and success. The book aims to inspire readers to take control of their finances and make smart decisions that will help them achieve their goals.

The idea for this book came to me after meeting the Sharma family. They faced financial difficulties due to poor financial planning and a lack of savings. However, I saw them use a plan that helped them manage their finances and save for the future.

In this book, I have shared their story, along with tips that can help anyone looking to improve their financial situation. From setting goals to creating a budget, from investing wisely to avoiding debt, this book covers everything you need to know to take control of your finances.

I hope that this book will help you on your own savings adventure and empower you to achieve financial stability and success. Remember, it's never too late to start saving, and every small step you take towards financial security is a step in the right direction.

Happy reading!
Dhandesh

INTRODUCTUCTION

Get ready to join the Sharma family on a journey through the ups and downs of financial instability in "The Great Indian Savings Adventure." The Sharmas, a middle-class family of four, resided in Tamil Nadu, India, where Mr. Sharma (Rudra Sharma) had been the sole breadwinner for over a couple of decades.

However, their world was shattered when the local factory where Rudra Sharma worked shut down due to financial issues. Suddenly, the Sharmas found themselves without a steady source of income and facing a harsh reality they were not prepared for.

They navigate the challenges of unemployment and financial instability. Mrs. Sharma (Anjali Sharma) tried to put on a brave face, reassuring her husband and children that they would figure something out. Rohit worried about his college education and did not want to burden his family.

Ria was concerned about her education and wanted to attend a good college. The Sharmas had to make sacrifices and adjustments to their lifestyle, cutting back on expenses, and finding part-time jobs to contribute to the family's income.

Despite their efforts, the Sharma family was still struggling to make ends meet. They had to make tough decisions like canceling their family vacation and considering downsizing their home. The Sharmas started to realize the value of money and the importance of financial planning. They had taken their comfortable lifestyle for granted and had not prepared for the possibility of a financial crisis.

As the Sharma family navigated their way through this financial crisis, they learned the importance of financial planning and investing. They became more proactive in their search for scholarships, grants, and part-time jobs. They also started to research ways to save and invest their money to secure their future.

In this compelling story, the Sharma family teaches us the value of perseverance, sacrifice, and financial planning in the face of adversity. "The Great Indian Savings Adventure" is a must-read for anyone facing financial instability and looking for inspiration to overcome it.

1. THE FAMILY CRISIS

Get ready to embark on a journey with the Sharma family - a middle-class family of four residing in Tamil Nadu, India. Rudra Sharma, the family's patriarch, had been the sole breadwinner for over a couple of decades, working hard at a local factory. However, his world was shattered when he received the devastating news that the factory was shut down due to financial issues.

With no warning, Rudra Sharma found himself without a job and no steady source of income. The news was a shock to the entire family, who had grown accustomed to a comfortable life without financial worries. Suddenly, they were forced to confront a harsh reality they were not prepared for.

Anjali Sharma (Mrs. Sharma) knew that her family was facing a difficult time, but she tried to put on a brave face. "Don't worry, we'll figure something out," she said to her husband and children.

"But how Ma?" asked Rohit. "College tuition is so expensive. I don't want to be a burden on you guys."

"I know it's tough, beta," Anjali Sharma replied, using the affectionate term for son. "But we'll find a way. Maybe you can apply for scholarships or grants."

Rohit nodded, but he still felt uncertain about his future. Meanwhile, Ria was also feeling the pressure of their financial situation. "What about my studies, Ma?" she asked. "I want to go to a good college too."

Anjali Sharma placed a comforting hand on her daughter's shoulder. "We want that for you too, beta. But we'll have to be more careful with our spending and see what options we have."

As the Sharmas discussed their options, they realized that they needed to make some sacrifices and adjustments to their lifestyle. It wouldn't be easy, but they were determined to overcome this obstacle together.

As the Sharma family struggled to come to terms with their sudden loss of income, they knew that they had to find a way to make ends meet. Ria was particularly worried about how they would afford her education.

"I don't want to be a burden on you guys," she said to her parents one evening. "But I want to go to college and make something of myself."

Anjali Sharma hugged her daughter tightly. "You will go to the college of your choice, beta," she said. "We'll find a way to make it work."

Rudra Sharma nodded in agreement. "I'm actively looking for a new job, but it might take some time. In the meantime, we'll have to be more careful with our spending."

Sharma Family started cutting back on their expenses, but they quickly realized that it wasn't enough. That's when Rohit stepped in with a more long-term solution.

"I've been doing some research," he said, "and I think I can apply for scholarships and grants to help pay for my college tuition. And I can also try to find a part-time job to contribute to the family's income."

THE GREAT INDIAN SAVINGS ADVENTURE

The Sharmas were impressed by Rohit's initiative and determination. They knew that they had a long road ahead of them, but they were willing to do whatever it took to achieve their dreams.

Ria also started to help out by tutoring younger students in her spare time. She enjoyed teaching, and it was a way for her to earn some extra money for her family.

Despite their efforts, the Sharma family was still struggling. They were constantly worried about how they would pay their bills and put food on the table. They knew that they needed to find a more sustainable solution to their financial crisis.

As the days went by, the Sharma family started to realize the value of money and the importance of financial planning. They had taken their comfortable lifestyle for granted and had not prepared for the possibility of a financial crisis.

some tough decisions, such as canceling their family vacation, and they were even considering downsizing their home.

Rudra Sharma was actively looking for a new job, but he was having a hard time finding one that paid as well as his previous job. He was willing to work any job, but he needed to find something that could support his family.

Anjali Sharma started to worry about their family's future. She knew that they needed to find a way to save and invest their money, but she didn't know where to start. She was determined to find a way to secure their future, and she started to research ways to do so.

Rohit and Ria also realized the gravity of their situation and started to take responsibility for their future. They started to learn about financial planning and investing, and they became more proactive in their search for scholarships and part-time jobs.

One day, while Anjali Sharma was out running errands, she bumped into an old friend, Charumathi whose husband worked at ICICI Bank as a manager. They started talking about their current situations, and Anjali Sharma shared the struggles that her family was going through.

As the days turned into weeks, the Sharma family's financial situation became increasingly dire. They had to make

Anjali Sharma: Hi Charumathi, it's been ages since we last met! How have you been?

Charumathi: Hey Anjali! I've been good, thanks for asking. How about you and your family?

Anjali Sharma: To be honest, we've been facing some financial struggles lately. It's been difficult to make ends meet.

Charumathi: I'm sorry to hear that. Have you considered talking to a financial advisor?

Anjali Sharma: Not really. We've never really thought about it.

Charumathi: Well, my husband works at ICICI Bank, and they offer free financial planning sessions to their customers. It could help you plan for your future.

Anjali Sharma: That sounds interesting. I'll consider it.

Sudheer (Charumathi's Husband): So Mrs. Sharma, tell me a little bit about your financial situation.

THE GREAT INDIAN SAVINGS ADVENTURE

Anjali Sharma: Well, we're facing some difficulties right now. Our expenses are high, and our income is not enough to cover everything.

Sudheer: I understand. Let's take a look at your current investments and see if we can optimize them. Have you considered mutual funds?

Anjali Sharma: No, we haven't.

Sudheer: Mutual funds are a great way to invest your money and get a good return. We can also set up a SIP (Systematic Investment Plan) for you, which means that you can invest a fixed amount of money every month.

Sudheer explained that mutual funds are professionally managed investment portfolios that pool money from multiple investors to purchase a diverse range of securities, such as stocks and bonds. By investing in mutual funds, investors can access a wide variety of securities that may not be available to them individually, and the risk is spread out across the entire portfolio.

He then went on to explain Systematic Investment Plan (SIP) as a way to invest in mutual funds. She explained that SIP is a method of investing a fixed amount of money regularly, typically every month, into a mutual fund. By investing regularly through SIP, investors can benefit from the power of compounding, which means that the returns earned on the investment are reinvested to generate further returns.

Sudheer emphasized that SIP is a great way to start investing in mutual funds as it is a disciplined investment approach, and it allows investors to take advantage of the power of compounding. She also explained that the amount invested through SIP can be varied as per the investor's financial goals and risk tolerance.

Mrs. Sharma was impressed with the concept of mutual funds and SIP and decided to invest in them to meet her family's long-term financial goals. The financial advisor helped her choose the right mutual fund schemes based on her financial goals and risk profile and also explained the process of investing through SIP.

Anjali Sharma: We've been making a lot of changes since we met with your husband Sudheer "Bhai".

Charumathi: That's great to hear! What changes have you made?

Anjali Sharma: We started investing in mutual funds and have set up a SIP. We also started an emergency fund and have cut back on unnecessary expenses.

Charumathi: That's fantastic! It sounds like you're on the right track.

Anjali Sharma: Yes, we're still facing some difficulties, but we're determined to overcome them.

As the Sharma family started to implement the financial advice given by the financial advisor Sudheer, they slowly started to see improvements in their financial situation. They continued to work hard and look for new opportunities to earn money. And with the support of Charumathi and her husband, they were able to navigate through their struggles and come out stronger. The Great Indian Savings Adventure is a story of hope and determination, showing how anyone can overcome their financial difficulties with the right mindset and guidance.

2. THE MONEY STRUGGLE BEGINS

Rohit and Ria noticed that their parents were always fighting about money, and they were worried about the impact it was having on their family. They wanted to help, but they didn't know how.

One day, Rohit came across an advertisement for a part-time job at a local restaurant. He thought it would be a great opportunity to earn some extra money and help his family. He talked to his parents about it, and they agreed that it was a good idea.

Ria was also looking for some other ways to contribute to the family's income. She started to research online about different jobs she could do from home. She found a website that offered freelance writing opportunities and applied for a job. To her surprise, she got hired and was able to start earning money from home.

Despite their efforts, the money struggles continued. The Sharmas was still having trouble paying their bills, and they were getting further and further into debt.

One evening, as the Sharmas sat down for dinner, Rudra Sharma broke the news that they might have to sell their house. Rohit and Ria were shocked and upset. They had grown up in that house, and it was the only home they had ever known.

Anjali was also devastated by the news. She had always dreamed of having a beautiful home, and she felt like a failure for not being able to provide for her family. She broke down in tears. She couldn't take the stress anymore, and she didn't know what they were going to do.

Rohit and Ria were heartbroken to see their mother so upset, and they knew that they had to do something to help. They started to look for more job opportunities and even thought about dropping out of school to work full-time.

One day, while Rohit was working at the restaurant, he overheard a conversation between two customers. They were talking about how they had invested in the stock market and made a lot of money. Rohit was intrigued and started to research more about the stock market.

He shared his findings with his sister Ria, who was also struggling to earn money.

Rohit: "Ria, have you ever heard about the stock market? I was listening to these customers at the restaurant, and they were talking about how they made a lot of money by investing in it."

Ria: "No, I haven't. But it sounds interesting. What did you find out?"

Rohit explained his research and how investing in stocks could potentially bring higher returns than their current investments in SIPs and mutual funds.

Ria: "That does sound promising. But we should talk to Mom and Dad about it. They're the ones who handle our investments."

Later that evening, Rohit and Ria sat down with their parents and discussed their idea of investing in the stock market. Their parents were hesitant at first, but they listened to their children and decided to do some research on their own.

Rudra: "We're already investing in SIP and Mutual Funds. Why do we need to invest in stocks?"

Rohit: "Dad, we need to try something new. We've been struggling with our finances even after investing in SIP and Mutual Funds. We need to explore other options to increase our returns."

Anjali: "I see your point, Rohit. But investing in stocks can be risky, and we don't want to lose our hard-earned money."

Ria: "But, Mom, with proper research and guidance, we can make informed decisions and minimize the risks."

The Sharmas started to invest in the stock market, and to their surprise, they started to see returns. They invested in companies that they believed in and did their research before making any decisions.

Over the next few weeks, the Sharma family became amateur stock market investors. They spent their evenings researching companies, reading financial reports, and tracking the performance of their investments.

At first, there were some ups and downs. Some of their investments performed well, while others didn't. But overall, they were making progress. Their investments were yielding returns, and they were able to pay off some of their debts.

Slowly but surely, their financial situation started to improve. They were able to pay off their debts, and they even started to save for their future.

Sharmas still had a long way to go, but they were no longer living in fear of losing their home. They had learned that with hard work and determination, they could overcome their financial struggles.

The Sharma family was feeling hopeful for the first time in a long time. They knew that investing in the stock market was no guarantee of financial success, but it was a start. They had taken a risk, and it was paying off.

"Sometimes, the greatest adventures are the ones we embark on to save our families. Rohit and Ria's journey into the stock market may have started as a last resort, but it became a path to financial freedom and hope. Their determination and courage remind us that even in the darkest of times, there is always a way to create a brighter future."

※ ※ ※

3. THE FAMILY MEETING

Mr. and Mrs. Sharma called a family meeting one evening after dinner. Rohit and Ria were curious as to what was going on, but they could sense that their parents were stressed.

As they all gathered in the living room, Rudra Sharma began to speak. "I know that things have been tough lately, and we're all feeling the pressure. But I think it's time that we come together as a family and figure out how we can make things better."

Anjali nodded in agreement. "Your father and I have been discussing our finances, and we need to start cutting back on our expenses and start saving money."

Rohit and Ria exchanged worried looks. They knew that their parents had been struggling, but they didn't realize just how dire the situation had become.

Rudra Sharma pulled out a sheet of paper and began to list off some of the family's expenses. "We need to start being more mindful of what we're spending. We can't afford to be going out to eat as much as we have been, and we need to start taking shorter showers to save on our water bill."

Ria raised her hand. "What about my tuition fees? I know they're expensive, but I need to finish school if I want to go to college."

Rudra Sharma looked at his daughter and nodded. "We're not going to sacrifice your education, Ria. We'll find a way to make it work."

The Sharmas continued to discuss their expenses, and they made a list of ways that they could cut back. They decided to cancel their cable subscription, start shopping at discount grocery stores, and carpool more often.

As the meeting came to a close, Anjali Sharma spoke up. "I know that this is going to be tough, but we can do it. We're a family, and we need to support each other."

Rohit and Ria nodded in agreement. They knew that they had to do their part to help their family through this difficult time.

Over the next few weeks, the Sharma family worked hard to stick to their budget. They started cooking meals at home instead of going out to eat, and they found ways to entertain themselves without spending money.

At first, it was difficult. They missed their cable TV shows and their weekend trips to the mall. But as time went on, they began to realize that they didn't need those things to be happy.

They started playing board games together, taking walks in the park, and having picnics in the backyard. They found that they enjoyed each other's company more than they enjoyed their material possessions.

As the days went by, the Sharma family began to implement the changes they had discussed during their family meeting. They stuck to their budget and found creative ways to save money.

Rohit and Ria were determined to do their part to help their family. The extra cash they were getting from their part-time jobs was adding up as their savings for their future education.

Rohit: "Wow, Oxford University! That's amazing, Ria. It's one of the best universities in the world."

Ria: "I know, right? I've been dreaming of studying there for years. But it's so expensive, and I don't want to burden our family with the cost."

Rohit: "I understand. But you're doing great in your studies, Ria. I'm sure you'll be able to get a scholarship."

Ria: "I hope so. That's why I'm working so hard. I want to make sure I get good grades and stand out from the other applicants."

Rohit: "I believe in you, Ria. You're smart, hardworking, and determined. You can achieve anything you set your mind to."

Ria: "Thanks, Rohit. That means a lot coming from you. You're always so supportive of my goals."

Rohit: "Of course, Ria. We're a team, and we have to help each other out. Besides, I know you'll do the same for me when it's my turn to chase my dreams."

Rudra also started looking for a new job. He spent hours every day searching online and networking with his contacts. He was determined to find a job that would help ease the family's financial burden.

Anjali took charge of the family's grocery shopping, and she found that shopping at discount stores and using coupons could save them a significant amount of money each week. She also started cooking more meals at home and packing lunches for Rohit and Ria instead of buying food at school.

As the weeks went by, the Sharma family's efforts began to pay off. They were spending less money each week, and they were starting to see some savings in their bank account.

One day, Anjali Sharma received a call from her husband while he was out networking. He had an interview with a company that he had been trying to get in touch with for weeks.

He rushed home and told his family about the interview. They all gathered around as he prepared for it, offering words of encouragement and support.

A few days later, Rudra Sharma received the news that he had been offered the job. The Sharmas were overjoyed, and they celebrated with a homemade dinner and a game of Monopoly.

As they sat around the table, Rudra Sharma raised a glass to his family. "I couldn't have done this without all of you. You all pulled together during our time of need, and I'm so proud of every one of you."

Rohit and Ria smiled, feeling proud of themselves as well. They had stepped up and helped their family during a difficult time, and they knew that they had grown as individuals because of it.

The Sharma family was in a much better place. They had faced a tough financial crisis, but they had come out on the other side stronger than ever before.

> "There was a sense of hope and inspiration. Sharma family worked together to overcome their struggles, and they knew that they too could face any challenges that came their way with the support of their loved ones."

✷✷✷

4. THE FAMILY'S MONEY-SAVING ATTEMPTS

As the Sharma family continued their efforts to save money and overcome their financial struggles, they realized that they needed to make some major changes to their spending habits.

Anjali Sharma took charge of the family's finances, creating a detailed budget and tracking all of their expenses. She also encouraged her family to start looking for ways to cut back on unnecessary expenses.

The first thing they did was to stop eating out at restaurants. Instead, they started cooking meals at home, which were not only cheaper but also healthier. Anjali Sharma started preparing meals in bulk and freezing them for later use, which saved them time and money.

They also stopped buying new clothes and started shopping for deals and using coupons. Ria and Rohit started to appreciate the value of second-hand clothing and began to shop at thrift stores. They found some great deals and even managed to score some designer clothes at a fraction of the cost.

To save on electricity bills, they turned off all the lights and appliances when not in use. They also started using energy-efficient light bulbs and installed a programmable thermostat to regulate the temperature in their home.

Rohit and Ria also did their part to save money. They started to walk or bike to school instead of taking the bus. They also started to bring their lunches to school instead of buying food from the cafeteria.

Rudra Sharma also decided to sell his old car, which needed repairs, and purchase a smaller, more fuel-efficient vehicle. This would save them money on gas and maintenance costs.

The Sharmas also decided to take on some DIY projects around the house. They learned how to fix leaky faucets and toilets, repaint their rooms, and even build their furniture. These projects not only saved them money but also gave them a sense of accomplishment.

As they began to make these changes, they noticed that their monthly bills were decreasing significantly. They were able to put the money they saved towards paying off their debts and increasing their savings.

One day, Rudra Sharma came across an advertisement for a financial advisor who was offering a free consultation. The Sharmas decided to take advantage of this opportunity and met with the advisor to discuss their finances.

The advisor was impressed with the family's efforts to save money and provided them with some valuable advice on how to manage their finances more effectively. He suggested that they create an emergency fund.

The Sharma family took the advisor's advice seriously and started putting a portion of their savings towards building an emergency fund.

As they continued to save money and manage their finances more effectively, the Sharma family began to feel more confident about their financial future. They had overcome their financial struggles through hard work and determination, and they were proud of their accomplishments.

Despite their efforts to save money, the Sharma family faced some challenges along the way. One of the biggest challenges was sticking to their budget.

Rohit was used to living a carefree life and found it difficult to adjust to the new changes. He missed going out with his friends and buying the latest gadgets. Anjali Sharma had to constantly remind him about their financial situation and the importance of sticking to their budget.

Ria, on the other hand, was more understanding and supportive of her parents' efforts. She tried to help in any way she could, even taking on extra chores around the house to save money on cleaning services.

Since beginning his new job, Rudra Sharma has grown somewhat accustomed to the routine tasks performed in the office. But he received a lower income than before, and he still has a month before receiving his first pay. The Sharma Family is responsible for paying his travel and eating expenses until then.

Since Rudra Sharma hasn't had a stable job, his debts have accumulated significantly. A few of the loans were past due. after a month, when the payment was received. The income the Sharma family was receiving was equal to the income and interest that needed to be paid.

As the Sharmas continued to save money and cut back on expenses, they realized that they needed to find new ways to increase their income. Rohit suggested that he start tutoring other students in his spare time too, while Ria offered to start selling some of her artwork online.

Anjali Sharma also came up with the idea of starting a small home-based business selling homemade snacks and sweets. She started advertising her products on social media and received a lot of orders. With the help of her children, she was able to start a successful small business that generated some extra income for the family.

As the Sharma family continued to work hard and make the necessary changes, they began to see the light at the end of the tunnel. They had started to save more money, increase their income and pay off their debts. They also learned valuable lessons about budgeting, saving and investing.

The Neighbour and their relatives were left feeling impressed and inspired by the Sharma family's determination to overcome their financial struggles. They had seen how a family can work together to achieve their goals and come out stronger on the other side.

"The Sharma family felt hopeful about their future. They knew that they still had a long way to go, but they were proud of their accomplishments and ready to face any challenges that came their way."

✳ ✳ ✳

5. THE INVESTMENT IDEA

The Sharma family had been doing everything they could to save money and increase their income. But they were still far from achieving their financial goals. Rohit, who had always been interested in finance and investments, began to explore different investment options.

Rohit was excited to share his investment ideas with his family. He had spent weeks researching and studying the stock market, and he was confident that he could help his family make some smart investment decisions.

At the family meeting, Rohit presented his findings. "I think we should invest in some good companies that have a history of steady growth," he said. "I have done some research and found some great options that we could consider."

Anjali was sceptical. "But how can we be sure that these companies will actually provide good returns on our investment in the future?" she asked.

"That's a valid concern," Rohit replied. "But I have looked at their past performance, their industry trends, and their financial statements. I believe they have a good chance of continuing to grow."

Rudra was also sceptical. "But what if the stock market crashes? We could lose all our money."

Rohit nodded. "Yes, that is a possibility. But we can mitigate the risk by diversifying our portfolio and investing in different sectors. That way, even if one company fails, we won't lose everything."

The Sharma family had a sizeable savings pool accumulated over the years from their investments in SIPs, the stock market, and bonds. After some discussions, they agreed to diversify their portfolio and invest a small portion of their savings in small companies and shops. They took the initiative to visit these companies and used contracts to buy some percentages of them in their name.

This move was a significant step in their investment journey, and they were all excited to see how it would turn out.

Rohit had done a lot of research on the best companies to invest in, and he helped his family choose some promising options. They also invested in "Anjali Sweets & Savouries", the homemade snacks business run by Anjali Sharma in getting new cutting-edge technologies in the area of making sweets and savouries.

Over time, the Sharmas started seeing positive returns on their investments. They got passive incomes monthly by investing in good companies and shops which was vastly researched by Rohit.

Anjali was pleased with the progress they had made. "I'm glad we listened to Rohit and took a chance on investing," she said. "We have been able to earn some extra income without doing anything."

Rudra agreed. "Yes, and it's good to know that we are also supporting small businesses by investing in them."

As their investments continued to grow, the Sharmas became more confident and excited about their financial future. They knew that there would be ups and downs in the stock market, but they felt secure knowing that they had made informed investment decisions.

"With Rohit's help and guidance, the Sharma family has found a way out of their financial crisis and has set themselves on the path to financial security. Investing is not about luck, it's about research and informed decisions"

✳ ✳ ✳

6. THE STOCK MARKET JOURNEY

The Sharma family is gaining more confidence in the investment process as they proceed with their stock market journey. Rohit spends time examining market movements and investigating various stocks, helping his family make informed decisions by keeping them updated on the status of their money.

As they continue on their journey, the Sharmas gains knowledge on the value of diversity and how to create a well-balanced portfolio. They begin to purchase a range of equities, including those from large-cap, mid-cap, and small-cap firms. Additionally, they start investing in exchange-traded funds (ETFs) and various mutual funds.

Rohit says, "Dad, we can expect a better return on investment (ROI) from ETFs than from mutual funds."

Anjali asks, "Beta, what are ETFs, and how do they give us better profits?"

Rohit explains, "ETFs (Exchange Traded Funds) are similar to individual stocks in the secondary markets that you can buy and sell. However, ETFs are designed to track the performance of a particular index."

Rudra asks, "You mean Nifty50 and Sensex?"

Rohit confirms, "Yes, Papa. ETFs track the performance of the companies under a specific index, which is a group of companies. By investing in ETFs, your portfolio is instantly diversified."

Anjali queries, "But isn't it like investing in one stock? How does it help with diversification?"

Rohit clarifies, "It's as if you have invested in all the companies under that particular index and not just one company, which reduces the risk. Even if one company doesn't perform well, others may perform better, resulting in a good profit. ETFs offer a better ROI compared to mutual funds."

Rudra says, "Hmm... That seems interesting. We invested the profit from TCS in Mom's business this week. Let's wait and see if we can earn profits elsewhere before we consider investing in ETFs."

The Sharma family experiences some market volatility, but they are prepared for it. They understand that investing requires patience and discipline and that the stock market is not a get-rich-quick scheme.

Rohit urges his family to approach investments in the long term. He explains that investing is crucial even when the market is down and that the stock market is cyclical. Additionally, he explains the principle of compounding and how reinvested dividends can help assets grow exponentially over time.

Rohit says, "Let me explain the principle of compounding to you, Mom and Dad. Reinvesting your dividends earns you interest on the interest you've already earned, which can help your assets grow exponentially over time."

Anjali Sharma asks, "That sounds interesting, but how does it work?"

Rohit responds, "Let me explain. If you invest Rs. 10,000 in a mutual fund with an average annual return of 10%, your investment would be worth Rs. 11,000 after one year. By reinvesting your dividends, you earn interest on the entire Rs. 11,000, not just the original Rs. 10,000. This can significantly help your investment grow over time."

Rudra Sharma adds, "I see what you mean. That's a powerful concept."

Rohit agrees, "Exactly. Reinvesting dividends is crucial to achieving your financial goals faster and more efficiently, which is why it's essential to have a long-term investment horizon."

❋ ❋ ❋

As their investments continue to increase, the Sharma family sets more challenging financial objectives. They discuss investing in real estate and saving for their children's college education, knowing that discipline and diligence can help them achieve anything.

The Sharma family faces challenges on their stock market journey, experiencing some losses along the way.

However, they learn from their mistakes and adjust their investment strategy accordingly, understanding that investing is a marathon, not a sprint. They stay focused on their long-term goals.

Throughout their journey, the Sharma family learns the value of financial literacy and the importance of working together to achieve their financial goals. They realize that with the right mindset and approach, anyone can attain financial security and freedom.

The family starts keeping a closer eye on their spending and creates a budget to stay on track. Rohit helps his parents set up a retirement account and encourages them to save for their golden years. He explains the benefits of compound interest and how saving a little bit every month can add up over time.

Additionally, the family discusses the importance of having an emergency fund. They understand that unexpected expenses can arise at any time, and having a financial cushion can help them weather any storm.

As the family becomes more financially savvy, they teach their friends and neighbour about the benefits of investing and saving. They hold informal meetings, share their experiences, and impart their newfound knowledge to others in their community.

The Sharma family's financial knowledge and discipline pay off in unexpected ways. They feel more secure and less stressed about their financial situation, enabling them to take a family vacation and plan for their future with confidence.

> **"The Sharma family reflects on their journey and the lessons they've learned. They realize that anyone can achieve financial security and freedom with a little effort and education. They are grateful for their journey and excited to see what the future holds."**

❈ ❈ ❈

7. THE SETBACK

The Sharma family wakes up one morning to the news that the stock market has crashed. They are horrified to see that the value of their investments has plummeted overnight. Rudra Sharma is crestfallen and starts to panic about their financial situation. Anjali Sharma tries to remain calm, but she can't hide her worry.

Rohit tries to reassure his parents that the stock market will eventually recover, but his words fall on deaf ears. The family is disheartened and feels like all their hard work and savings have gone to waste.

As the days pass, the Sharma family tries to come to terms with their loss. They start to argue and blame each other for their financial troubles. The tension in the household is palpable, and it seems like their financial goals are slipping further and further away.

However, Rohit refuses to give up. He knows that setbacks are a part of investing, and he's determined to get his family back on track. He spends long hours researching the market and talking to financial experts to find a way out of their current predicament.

Finally, Rohit comes up with a plan. He proposes that the family hold onto their stocks and ride out the market downturn. He explains that selling their investments now would only solidify their losses, and it's better to wait for the market to recover.

At first, the rest of the family is hesitant to go along with Rohit's plan. They fear that they will lose even more money if they hold onto their investments. But Rohit is persistent, and he shows them data and research that supports his proposal.

"Finally, the family agrees to hold onto their stocks and weather the storm. They take a deep breath and try to remain patient as the market slowly starts to recover."

✸✸✸

Rohit is particularly disheartened by the setback. He had put a lot of effort into researching and investing in the stock market, and now it all seemed like a waste. Rudra and Anjali Sharma try to console him and remind him that setbacks are a part of any investment journey. They explain that while it's important to be cautious, they can't let one setback discourage them from pursuing their financial goals.

The family takes some time to regroup and reflect on what went wrong with their investment. They realize that they were too focused on short-term gains and didn't consider the long-term prospects of the companies they invested in. Rohit takes it upon himself to learn more about investment strategies and risk management.

He spends hours researching and reading books about investing, and he even enrol in an online course on financial planning. His dedication pays off, and he develops a more sophisticated understanding of the stock market.

Eventually, Rohit comes up with a new investment plan that is more diversified and focused on long-term growth. The Sharmas are uncertain at first, but they trust Rohit's research and decide to give it a try.

Over time, the family's investments start to grow again. They continue to make careful investments and monitor the stock market closely. Rohit even starts to develop a passion for investing and decides to pursue a career in finance.

"The family is proud of their progress and happy that they didn't let one setback discourage them from pursuing their financial goals. "They realize that building wealth takes time, patience, and dedication, but the rewards are worth it. They also realize that financial literacy and planning are essential for achieving financial stability and success."

8. THE COMEDY OF ERRORS

After the setback of losing a significant portion of their investment, the Sharma family is determined to figure out what went wrong and try to salvage what they can. They start by doing more research on the stock market and consulting with financial advisors.

However, as they delve deeper into the world of investments, they find themselves making several comical mistakes. For instance, Anjali Sharma mistakenly invests in a company that she thought was a reputable tech giant but turns out to be a small start-up with no real prospects. Meanwhile, Rudra Sharma invests all of their remaining funds into a single stock, hoping for a quick return on investment.

To make matters worse, Rohit and Ria start to get involved in the investment process as well, and their lack of experience leads to even more errors. They invest in companies based solely on their names and forget to diversify their portfolio.

Despite the series of missteps, the Sharma family tries to keep their spirits up and even finds humour in their mistakes. They joke about investing in a company that produces eco-friendly toothbrushes, only to find out that no one wants to buy them.

Their comical errors and the ensuing laughter bring a sense of lightness to their otherwise stressful financial situation. The family starts to realize that they don't have to take themselves too seriously and that it's okay to make mistakes as long as they learn from them.

As the family continues to navigate the stock market with a newfound sense of humour, they start to make smarter investment decisions. They diversify their portfolio and invest in companies with a proven track record, rather than just going for the latest trends.

The family also starts to bond over their shared experiences and a newfound appreciation for financial literacy. They have open discussions about money and investments, and Rohit and Ria start to understand the importance of financial planning and long-term investment goals.

"The Sharma family has learned to take their investments seriously, but not themselves. Their comical errors have brought them closer together and helped them become more financially savvy."

❋ ❋ ❋

The family's attempts at fixing their investment mistakes were both humorous and frustrating. They made a few misguided decisions, such as investing in companies that they knew little about, and as a result, their investment suffered. In one instance, Rohit invested in a company that he thought was a fast-growing tech firm, but it turned out to be a grocery store chain.

One evening, gathered around the dining table, Rohit, Ria, Anjali, and Rudra couldn't help but chuckle at their past blunders. The room echoed with laughter as they recounted their most memorable investment errors.

Rohit, always the adventurous one, started the conversation with a sheepish grin. "Remember that time when I invested in what I thought was a booming tech company? Turns out, it was a grocery store chain! I thought I'd be coding, but instead, I ended up bagging groceries in my imagination!"

The family erupted into laughter, imagining Rohit amidst stacks of canned goods and vegetables instead of writing code. Ria chimed in, "And let's not forget when I invested in that eco-friendly toothbrush company. We thought we'd revolutionize dental hygiene, but it turned out no one wanted to buy a toothbrush made from recycled materials!"

Anjali joined the fun, sharing her own mishap. "Oh, the time I invested in what I thought was a reputable tech giant! Imagine my surprise when I discovered it was a tiny start-up with big dreams but no actual prospects. I guess I fell for their fancy website and catchy tagline!"

Rudra couldn't help but laugh along with his family. "And here I thought diversifying meant randomly buying stocks without any research! I once invested in a pharmaceutical company that was being investigated for fraud. Talk about diversifying my risk!"

As their laughter subsided, they realized that their comical errors had brought them closer as a family. They found comfort in their shared mistakes and the ability to laugh at themselves. The Sharma family understood that making mistakes was a part of the learning process.

Rudra Sharma's attempts to diversify the family's investment were equally comical. He invested in a variety of stocks without fully understanding their potential risks or benefits. In one instance, he bought shares in a pharmaceutical company only to find out later that the company was under investigation for fraud.

Despite their mistakes, the Sharma family persevered and continued to learn about the stock market. They read books, watched videos, and talked to experts to gain a better understanding of how the market works.

Their efforts began to pay off when they made their first profitable investment. The Sharmas were ecstatic and celebrated by going out for a nice meal. The small victory gave them hope and renewed their drive to continue investing.

As they continued to invest, the family became more cautious and aware of potential risks. They diversified their portfolio, investing in a mix of stocks, mutual funds, and government securities. They also set clear goals and created a budget to ensure that they were saving and investing enough to reach their targets.

Looking back on their journey, the Sharma family realized that their initial setbacks and comical mistakes were just part of the learning process. They learned to be patient, to do their research, and to take calculated risks. Above all, they learned that with determination and hard work, they could overcome financial obstacles and achieve their goals.

"The family's journey in the stock market was far from over, but they were better equipped to handle the ups and downs of investing. They looked forward to the future with renewed optimism and a newfound appreciation for the power of savings and investment."

✻ ✻ ✻

9. THE TURNING POINT

The Sharma family had been through a lot of ups and downs in their journey to financial stability. They had lost a significant portion of their investment due to the stock market crash, and their mistakes had cost them dearly. However, they refused to give up on their dreams of a better future, and this led them to a turning point in their lives.

After the crash, Rohit took it upon himself to learn more about the stock market and investment strategies. He spent hours researching and reading books on the subject, and he shared his newfound knowledge with the rest of the family. They learned about diversification, risk management, and long-term investing. They also realized that their earlier mistakes were due to a lack of knowledge and not understanding the market.

Amidst the ups and downs of the stock market, the Sharma family discovered a silver lining in the form of their small venture, Anjali Sweets & Savouries. As they weathered their share market struggles, their entrepreneurial endeavour began to flourish and provide a much-needed source of income. It became a symbol of resilience and a testament to their ability to adapt and find opportunities in challenging times.

The business grew steadily, gaining popularity within the community. The aroma of freshly made Jalebis and samosas wafted through the air, drawing customers from far and wide. Anjali's dedication to quality and authenticity ensured that her creations stood out, captivating the taste buds of every customer who walked through their doors.

One evening, as the family sat together, savoring a plate of their famous Gulab Jamuns, they reflected on their journey. Rudra broke the silence, his voice filled with gratitude. "Who would have thought that our little venture would become such a success? Anjali, your sweets have become a sensation in the neighbourhood!"

Anjali blushed, humbled by her husband's praise. "It's all thanks to your support and the love of our customers. I can't believe how far we've come since those initial days of struggling in the stock market."

Rohit, with a sense of pride, chimed in, "You know, Dad, I think our small business was a crucial investment for us. It provided a stable source of income when the stock market was volatile."

Ria nodded in agreement, her eyes gleaming with excitement. "And remember those real estate investments we made? They turned out to be a lifesaver during the market crash. We were able to rely on the passive income they generated."

As they educated themselves, the Sharmas also started to look at their finances more closely. They tracked their expenses and created a budget, which helped them to cut back on unnecessary expenses. They also started to save money regularly, setting aside a portion of their income each month.

The family's newfound knowledge and financial discipline paid off in unexpected ways. They started to see positive returns on their investments, and their savings started to grow. The stress and tension caused by the financial crisis began to ease, and they started to feel more confident about their future.

As they continued to learn and grow, the Sharma family also started to explore other avenues of investment. They looked into SIPs, real estate, and other investment options, all the while keeping their focus on long-term growth and stability.

Through their journey, the Sharma family learned that financial stability was not just about making money but also about managing it wisely. They learned that with the right knowledge and discipline, anyone could achieve their financial goals, even in the face of adversity.

The major learning for the Sharma family was not just a financial one, but also a personal one. They had grown closer as a family through their shared struggles and successes. They had learned to work together, support each other, and celebrate each other's achievements.

As they looked back on their journey, the Sharma family realized that their financial crisis had been a blessing in disguise. It forced them to reevaluate their priorities and take control of their finances. It brought them closer together and taught them valuable lessons that would stay with them for a lifetime.

The Sharma family began their journey of learning about the stock market and financial management. They started attending seminars and workshops to understand the intricacies of investing in the stock market. Rohit and Ria took online courses on personal finance and investment management. They even started reading books on the subject and watching videos on YouTube.

Some Books that they read were :

1) "The Intelligent Investor" by Benjamin Graham

2)"A Random Walk Down Wall Street" by Burton Malkiel

3) "Coffee Can Investing: The Low-Risk Road to Stupendous Wealth" by

Saurabh Mukherjea and Pranab Uniyal

4) "Value Investing and Behavioral Finance: Insights into Indian Stock

THE GREAT INDIAN SAVINGS ADVENTURE

Market Realities" by Prasanna Chandra

5) "The Thoughtful Investor" by Basant Maheshwari

The family learned about the importance of diversifying their portfolio, investing in blue-chip companies, and staying up-to-date with market trends. They also learned about the significance of creating a financial plan and setting financial goals for the future.

Slowly but surely, the family started to see the results of their efforts. They diversified their portfolio and invested in different sectors. They monitored their investments and adjusted their strategy according to market trends.

They also created a budget and stuck to it, cutting back on unnecessary expenses.

Their hard work and dedication paid off, and they started to see positive returns on their investments. The family's financial situation started to improve, and they were able to pay off their debts and save for the future.

"The Sharma family learned that the stock market is not a get-rich-quick scheme, but rather a long-term investment strategy that requires patience, dedication, and knowledge. They learned that investing is not gambling but rather a calculated risk that can provide financial stability and security in the long run."

❋ ❋ ❋

It was a turning point for the Sharma family, as they shifted their mindset from short-term gains to long-term financial planning. They realized that financial management is a continuous process that requires discipline, patience, and commitment.

As the family continued to learn and grow, they felt empowered to take control of their financial future. They were no longer living paycheck to paycheck, but rather creating a financial legacy for themselves and future generations.

"The Sharma family's journey serves as an inspiration to others struggling with financial instability. By educating themselves and implementing sound financial strategies, they were able to turn their financial crisis into a financial opportunity."

10. A SWEET SUCCESS

Anjali Sweets & Savouries played a significant role in the Sharma family's success. The small venture they started during their struggles became a pillar of strength during the challenging times of the stock market crash. The passive income generated by Anjali Sweets & Savouries provided a cushion, ensuring financial stability for the family when the market seemed uncertain.

The aroma of their famous products, including Jalebis, Gulab Jamuns, Palkova, Samosas, Cashew nut Pakodas, Fried Cashew Nuts, Salted Potato Chips, and more, filled the air, captivating the taste buds of their loyal customers. The mouthwatering treats became synonymous with quality and authenticity, attracting a growing customer base.

Word of mouth spread like wildfire, and soon people from far and wide began approaching Anjali Sweets & Savouries, seeking the opportunity to become distributors. The family's hard work, dedication, and commitment to delivering the finest sweets and savouries had paid off, establishing Anjali Sweets & Savouries as a brand to reckon with.

With their growing success, the Sharmas decided to rebrand their business as "Anjali Sweets." The new name symbolized their evolution and their commitment to maintaining the highest standards of taste and quality.

Anjali Sweets quickly became a household name in the South Indian states of Tamil Nadu, Bangalore, Kerala, Andhra Pradesh, and Telangana, and even made its mark in some parts of Maharashtra.

The family's entrepreneurial success didn't go unnoticed. Many heavyweight investors expressed interest in joining hands with Anjali Sweets, recognizing its potential to become a national brand. The Sharmas carefully evaluated these opportunities, ensuring that they aligned with their values and long-term vision.

The stock market, which was once a source of struggle and errors, had now become a significant source of profits for the Sharma family. Their diversified portfolio, guided by their newfound financial knowledge, yielded consistent returns. The lessons they had learned from their earlier mistakes had transformed them into savvy investors.

Their real estate investments also flourished, as they built nine houses that provided a steady stream of rental income. The local businesses they had invested in thrived as well, generating profits equivalent to the income Rudra had earned in his previous factory employment.

This financial success paved the way for Rohit and Ria to pursue their dreams. Rohit, with his growing expertise in finance through online courses, took charge of managing the various businesses the Sharmas were involved in. His dedication and strategic vision ensured their continued growth and success.

Ria, on the other hand, played an integral role in her mother's business. Her creativity and passion for baking helped introduce new and innovative products to the Anjali Sweets range, captivating the taste buds of their customers and keeping them coming back for more.

Ria's talent and hard work did not go unnoticed, as she earned a scholarship to study at Oxford University, a remarkable opportunity to further develop her skills and broaden her horizons.

As Ria delved into her studies, she found herself surrounded by peers from diverse backgrounds, each with their own unique stories and ambitions. The exchange of ideas and perspectives broadened her horizons and challenged her to think beyond the confines of her previous experiences.

Back home, Rohit continued to manage the various businesses the Sharma family had ventured into. His dedication and commitment to their financial growth were unwavering. With each passing day, his expertise in finance grew, and he became a trusted advisor not just to his family but also to other aspiring entrepreneurs seeking guidance.

Under Rohit's leadership, Anjali Sweets expanded its reach beyond South India, capturing the hearts and taste buds of people across the nation. The business became a beacon of success, showcasing the Sharma family's ability to turn adversity into opportunity.

Their real estate investments continued to bear fruit as well, with the rental income from the nine houses providing a steady stream of passive income. It was a testament to their astute financial decisions and long-term planning.

The local businesses they had invested in flourished, supporting the local economy and creating employment opportunities. The Sharma family's commitment to uplifting their community through their ventures became a source of pride and inspiration for others.

As the years passed, the Sharma family's wealth grew steadily. However, they never lost sight of the lessons they had learned during their challenging times. They remained humble, grounded, and committed to giving back to society.

After some years passed, One fine afternoon as the sun began to set, casting a warm glow over the Sharma family's backyard, they gathered around a table filled with a mouthwatering feast from Anjali Sweets. The tantalizing aroma of freshly cooked delicacies wafted through the air, enhancing the joyous atmosphere.

Rudra raised his glass, filled with a Coca-Cola, and cleared his throat to start the conversation. "My dear family, let us take a moment to reflect on our journey—the highs, the lows, and the incredible growth we've experienced together. We have come a long way from the days of struggle and uncertainty."

Anjali smiled, her eyes filled with pride. "Yes, my love. We faced our fair share of challenges, but we never gave up. Our determination to provide a better life for our family led us on this remarkable adventure."

Rohit, with a sense of gratitude in his voice, chimed in, "And look at where we are now. Our businesses have flourished, our investments have thrived, and our dreams are becoming a reality. It's a testament to our hard work and the power of saving and investing wisely."

Ria, her face glowing with excitement, added, "And let's not forget the impact we've had on the community. Through Anjali Sweets, we have not only brought joy to people's lives with our delectable treats but also created opportunities for others to thrive."

Rudra raised his glass higher, his eyes gleaming with happiness. "To our journey, to the lessons learned, and to the beautiful future that lies ahead! Cheers!"

The clinking of glasses resonated through the air as they toasted their achievements. The Sharma family basked in the warmth of their success, cherishing the bond they had built and the dreams they had turned into reality.

Anjali spoke softly, her voice filled with gratitude. "As I look at each of you, I am reminded of the strength we found in one another during the toughest of times. Our unity, resilience, and unwavering support have been the cornerstone of our success."

Rohit nodded, his eyes filled with determination. "Let us never forget the lessons we have learned-lessons of financial discipline, of taking calculated risks, and of never losing sight of our dreams. These lessons will guide us as we continue to grow and make a difference."

Ria, her voice filled with hope, added, "And let us also remember the importance of giving back. As we thrive, let's extend our hand to those who may still be on their own savings adventure, offering them support and encouragement along the way."

The evening sky painted a beautiful canvas above them, reminding the Sharma family of the endless possibilities that lay before them. They laughed, shared stories, and savoured each bite of the delicious food, knowing that their happiness was the result of their collective efforts.

As the night grew darker, they sat together, a family bound by love and shared accomplishments. They knew that their journey in The Great Indian Savings Adventure would be an eternal one—a story they would pass down to future generations, inspiring them to chase their dreams and secure their financial future.

"And so, under the starry sky, the Sharma family continued their celebration, grateful for their blessings, and excited for the adventures that awaited them. With hearts full of joy and a shared sense of purpose, they raised their glasses one more time, toasting love, success, and the never-ending pursuit of dreams."

AFTERWARDS

As Ria and Rohit grew up, they witnessed their parents struggle with finances. But they never let that dampen their spirits. They learned the value of hard work and determination from their parents and strived to achieve their dreams.

Ria pursued her passion for education and went to Oxford University to study. On the other hand, Rohit took over the snacks business and worked tirelessly to make it a success. Their efforts paid off, and they made their family proud.

Today, the Sharma family is no longer struggling with financial problems. Ria and Rohit's hard work and dedication have borne fruit, and they have created a better life for themselves and their family. The journey has been tough, but they have emerged stronger, wiser, and more resilient.

As they look back, they realize that their experiences have taught them invaluable lessons that they will cherish forever. They are grateful for the challenges they faced, for it made them who they are today.

EPILOGUE

As I reflect on the incredible journey of the Sharma family, I am filled with a deep sense of admiration and pride. Ria's pursuit of higher education at Oxford University and Rohit's successful takeover of the Anjali Sweets are a testament to their hard work and determination.

Through their savings adventure, the Sharmas not only overcame their financial crisis but also laid the foundation for a secure future. By adopting a disciplined approach to money management and making prudent investments, they have set themselves on a path to financial independence.

But their journey does not end here. The lessons learned along the way will continue to guide them as they navigate the challenges and opportunities of the future.

As Dhandesh, I hope that the Sharma family's story has inspired and empowered you to embark on your own savings adventure. Remember, every journey begins with a single step, and every step counts. With patience, persistence, and a little bit of courage, you too can achieve financial freedom and live the life of your dreams.

Thank you for joining me on this adventure, and I wish you all the best in your own pursuit of financial security.

Yours truly, Dhandesh

ABOUT THE AUTHOR

DHANDESH (DHANDESHWARAN K S) is an accomplished writer with a passion for personal finance and investment. With a couple years of experience in the finance industry, Dhandesh has helped countless individuals achieve their financial goals through sound advice and practical strategies.

Through this book, "The Great Indian Savings Adventure," Dhandesh shares their wealth of knowledge and insights into the world of saving and investing in India. As a writer, Dhandesh has a talent for explaining complex financial concepts in an accessible and engaging way, making this book a must-read for anyone looking to take control of their finances and secure their financial future.

www.ingramcontent.com/pod-product-compliance
Lightning Source LLC
Chambersburg PA
CBHW040329220526
45473CB00009B/2616